I Know That!

KU-320-511

How to Stay Healthy

Claire Llewellyn

W

FRANKLIN WATTS

LONDON•SYDNEY

DUDLEY PUBLIC LIBRARIES

L

687546   SCH

J613

First published in 2005 by Franklin Watts
96 Leonard Street, London EC2A 4XD

Franklin Watts Australia
Level 17/207 Kent Street, Sydney NSW 2000

Text copyright © Claire Llewellyn 2005
Design and concept © Franklin Watts 2005

Series adviser: Gill Matthews, non-fiction literacy
    consultant and Inset trainer
Series editor: Rachel Cooke
Series design: Peter Scoulding
Editor: Sarah Ridley
Designer: Jemima Lumley
Acknowledgements: Ingram Publishing/Alamy Images 13; Graham Bool Photography 10; Chris
Fairclough 12, 15b, 18, 19; Ray Moller cover, 4, 5, 6, 7t, 9r, 11, 14, 16, 17, 22, 23l; Steve Shott
title page, imprint page, 7b, 8, 9l, 15t, 20, 21, 23br.

Thanks to our models: Eliza, Harry, Joe, Luke, Nicholas, Reece, the Collins family and Dr J Ovuike.
Thanks also to Mrs Tarpey and St John's Green School for their help with the photography.

All rights reserved. No part of this publication may be reproduced, stored in a retrieval system, or
transmitted in any form or by any means, electronic, mechanical, photocopy, recording or
otherwise, without the prior written permission of the copyright owner.

A CIP catalogue record for this book is available from the British Library.

ISBN: 0 7496 6364 2

Dewey decimal classification number: 613

Printed in Malaysia

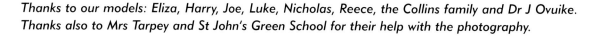

Contents

Good health

It is good to be healthy. Healthy people feel well and have lots of energy.

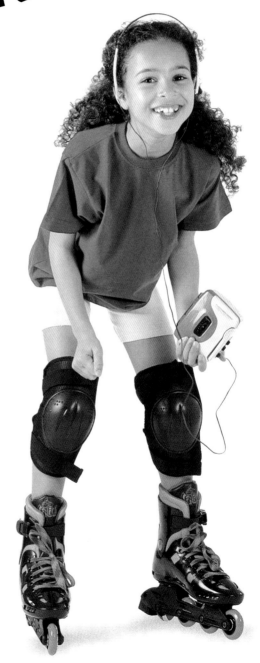

▶ *This girl feels healthy and happy.*

▼ Healthy people have plenty of energy – for work and for play.

How do you feel when you are ill?

5

Food for health

We need food to keep us healthy. Different foods help us in different ways.

▶ *These foods help our bodies to grow.*

◀ *These foods give us energy.*

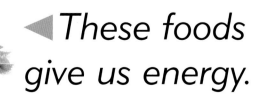

▼ *These foods help us to fight illness.*

What have you eaten today? It is good to eat a mixture of the types of food shown in these photos.

► *These foods make our bones and teeth strong.*

A healthy diet

We need to eat as many different foods as we can. This gives us a healthy diet.

◀ *We should try to eat five portions of fruit or vegetables a day. They might look like this.*

▼ *Drink plenty of water. It helps the body to work well.*

How many different foods have you eaten today?

▼ *Try to eat fewer sugary foods. Choose fruit instead.*

9

Exercise is good for us

Exercise helps us to stay healthy. It is very good for our bodies.

▶ *Exercise makes our bones stronger. It makes our heart and lungs work harder.*

Exercise uses our muscles and makes them stronger.

What happens to your body when you do fast exercise? Do you notice any changes?

11

Keep active

People exercise in many different ways.

▲ *You exercise your body just by walking around.*

▼ *Swimming lessons are a fun way to exercise with your friends.*

What kind of exercise do you enjoy? When do you do it?

Wash away germs

Invisible things called germs live on and in our bodies. Some of them can harm us.

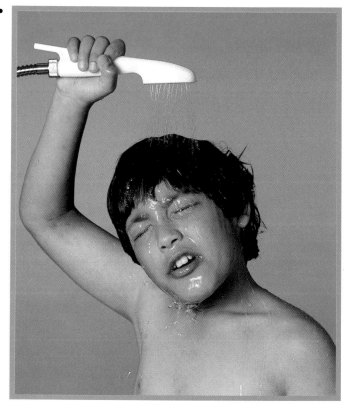

▶ *Washing helps to get rid of germs and makes us smell good, too.*

14

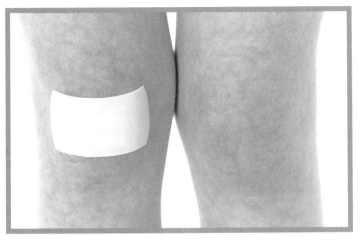 We should keep cuts clean, and protect them from germs.

► Some germs rot our teeth. We need to brush them away.

Always brush your teeth twice a day. Visit your dentist twice a year.

Stop germs spreading

Certain germs can make you ill. It is important to try and stop them from spreading.

▶ *Wash your hands before you eat and when you have been to the toilet.*

Use a tissue when you sneeze.

Some germs
can upset your
tummy. Others
spread coughs
and colds.

Feeling ill

Everyone feels ill at one time or another. When we do, we need to rest.

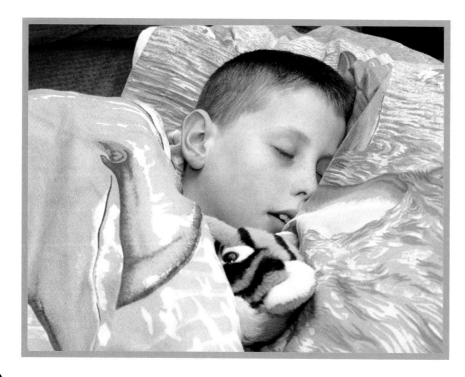

◄ *Sometimes our body gets better by itself. All it needs is rest.*

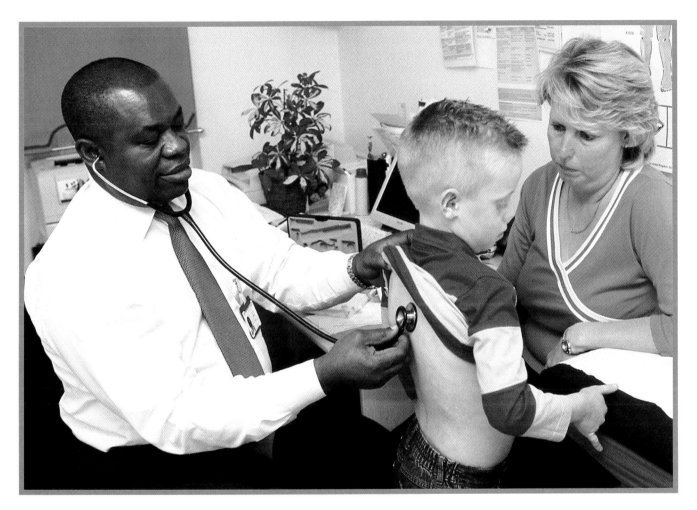

▲ *Sometimes we need to see a doctor.*

Sleep and rest are good for
the body. How many hours
do you sleep at night?

19

Taking the medicine

Sometimes doctors give us medicines. These help us to get better.

▶ *Medicines are very strong. We only need to take a little.*

▼ *Medicines often look like sweets or drinks. Take care not to eat medicines by mistake.*

Sweets and milk drink

Medicines

Can you tell them apart?

Never take medicine unless your parents or a doctor gives it to you.

When was the last time you took medicine?

I know that...

1 Healthy people feel well and have lots of energy.

2 Food helps the body in many ways.

3 We need to eat many different kinds of food.

4 Exercise is good for the body.

5 It is important to keep active.

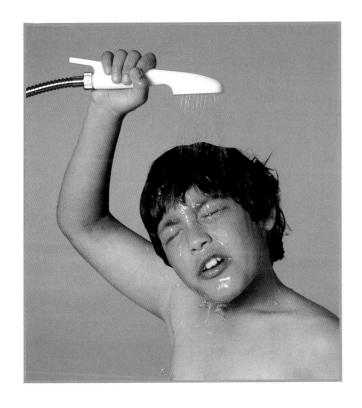

6 Keeping clean helps to get rid of germs and makes you smell good, too.

7 Washing our hands and using a tissue stop germs spreading.

8 When we feel ill, we need to rest.

9 Medicine helps us fight illness. Never take medicine unless a grown-up gives it to you.

23

Index

About this book

I Know That! is designed to introduce children to the process of gathering information and using reference books, one of the key skills needed to begin more formal learning at school. For this reason, each book's structure reflects the information books children will use later in their learning career – with key information in the main text and additional facts and ideas in the captions. The panels give an opportunity for further activities, ideas or discussions. The contents page and index are helpful reference guides.

The language is carefully chosen to be accessible to children just beginning to read. Illustrations support the text but also give information in their own right; active consideration and discussion of images is another key referencing skill. The main aim of the series is to build confidence – showing children how much they already know and giving them the ability to gather new information for themselves. With this in mind, the *I know that...* section at the end of the book is a simple way for children to revisit what they already know as well as what they have learnt from reading the book.